CONTENTS

W9-BYA-095

ANCIENT BRITAIN

The earliest evidence of humans in Britain was found at Happisburgh, in Norfolk. While no bones were found, **flint** tools and footprints found on the beach were made by an early human species. The first fossil evidence of early humans was a leg bone and two teeth found at Boxgrove, West Sussex, believed to be around 500,000 years old. The first evidence of our modern species of human was a jaw fragment found at Kent's Cavern, Devon. It is believed to be around 40,000 years old.

An ancient flint hand-ax found at Boxgrove.

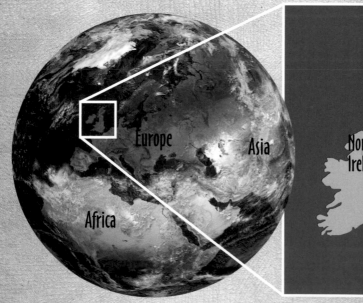

Africa   Europe   Asia

Scotland

Northern Ireland   BRITAIN

Wales   England

Timeline
A colored band by the page number shows each site's time period

500,000-c 5000 BCE	5000 - 2000 BCE	2000 - 800 BCE	800 - 150 BCE
Stone Age	First Farmers	Bronze Age	Iron Age

UNCOVERING THE CULTURE OF
ANCIENT BRITAIN

By Alix Wood

PowerKiDS
press
NEW YORK

Published in 2016 by
The Rosen Publishing Group, Inc.
29 East 21st Street, New York, NY 10010

Cataloging-in-Publication Data

Wood, Alix.
Uncovering the culture of ancient Britain / by Alix Wood.
p. cm. — (Archaeology and ancient cultures)
Includes index.
ISBN 978-1-5081-4647-6 (pbk.)
ISBN 978-1-5081-4648-3 (6-pack)
ISBN 978-1-5081-4649-0 (library binding)
1. Great Britain — Antiquities — Juvenile literature. 2. Great Britain — History — Juvenile literature.
I. Wood, Alix. II. Title.
DA90.W66 2016
914.2'03'1—d23
Copyright © 2016 Alix Wood Books

Editor: Eloise Macgregor
Designer: Alix Wood
Consultant: Rupert Matthews

Photo Credits: Cover, 1 © Shutterstock; 2, 8 bottom, 9 top, 13 top, 14 main image, 15, 26-27 bottom
© DollarPhotoClub; 3 top © Midnightblueowl; 4 top © M. S. Emmet; 4 bottom © Cresswell Crags
Museum; 6 main © Gary Troughton; 6 inset © Isabelle de Groote/Natural History Museum; 7 top ©
Simon Parfitt; 7 bottom, 23 top, 26 bottom left, 27 top © Trustees of the British Museum; 9 bottom ©
National Museums Scotland; 10 top © Robert McAdam; 11 top © Robert Paul Young; 12 bottom ©
Mike Lyons; 13 bottom right © Jim Champion; 14 inset © Joseph Lertola; 16 © Howard Smith; 17 top
© Howard Smith/Lynn Museum; 17 bottom © Picture Esk; 18 top, 19 © Dan McGregor; 18 bottom
© Willie Angus; 20 © National Museum Wales; 21 top © Ken Lewis; 21 bottom © Wolfgang Sauber/
Llangollen Museum; 22, 23 middle and bottom © Tom Sheldon; 24 bottom © Loz Pycock; 25 top ©
Keith Gough; 25 middle and bottom © Gnomonic; 26 top © Adam Cuerden; 28 top © Ad Meskens; 28
bottom © iStock; 29 top © Matthew Kirkland

Manufactured in the United States of America

CPSIA Compliance Information: Batch #: BW16PK For Further Information contact Rosen Publishing, New York, New York at 1-800-237-9932

Over the centuries, people in Britain began to form communities and to farm the land. Burial places built by these early farming communities are some of the oldest surviving buildings in the country. Wayland's Smithy (above) is a **long barrow** and chamber tomb in Oxfordshire. Inside, **archaeologists** found the jumbled remains of several adults and children. Some of the skeletons had suffered violent deaths. They may have been killed during a battle.

According to legend, if a traveler's horse has lost a shoe, if they leave the animal and a silver coin on top of Wayland's Smithy, when they return the next morning, the horse will have a new horseshoe and the money will be gone!

horse's mane

nostril

Artifact Facts

This bone has one of the oldest known carvings in Britain on it. Look at the center of the bone. There is a drawing of a horse's head. It was found in a cave in Derbyshire, and is believed to have been carved 12,500 years ago!

150 BCE- 43 CE	43-410 CE
Celtic	Roman

FOOTPRINTS IN THE SAND

Happisburgh

In 2010, several ancient flint tools were found on a beach at Happisburgh, Norfolk. The tools were over 800,000 years old! They are the oldest evidence of humans living in Britain. Later, in May 2013, a series of early human footprints were found on the same beach after very rough seas. The footprints could clearly be seen in a newly exposed layer of mud. Archaeologists had to work quickly to record the footprints before the tide washed them away. They were dated as coming from the same period as the flint tools, and are the oldest known early human footprints found outside Africa!

Experts at John Moores University joined together digital photographs to make this three-dimensional record of one of the footprints.

The cliffs at Happisburgh are gradually being worn away by the sea, changing the shape of the coastline.

A photograph of the footprints before they were washed away. The prints were made by a group of adults and children, walking along what would have then been a river's edge, almost one million years ago!

After the footprints were discovered, experts had to work quickly at low tide, often in pouring rain, to record images of all the prints. Because of the softness of the mud, within two weeks the footprints had been destroyed. Approximately fifty footprints were found. It is believed that they were made by the species *Homo antecessor*, known to have lived in Spain around 800,000 years ago. Archaeologists believe the group may have been searching the **mudflats** for seafood such shellfish or crabs. When the footprints were made, the river ran along a grassy valley surrounded by pine forests. **Extinct** animals such as mammoth and saber-toothed cats would have lived in the area!

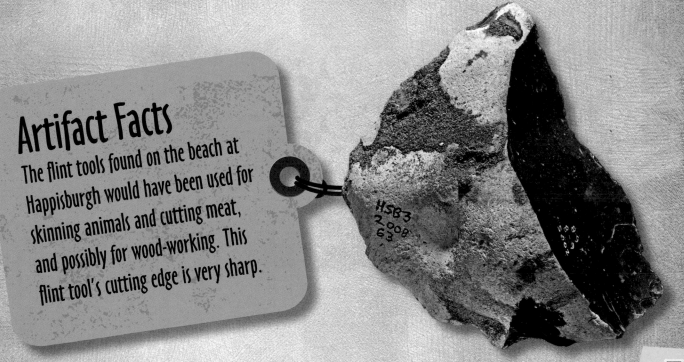

Artifact Facts
The flint tools found on the beach at Happisburgh would have been used for skinning animals and cutting meat, and possibly for wood-working. This flint tool's cutting edge is very sharp.

HSB3
2008
63

SKARA BRAE

Skara Brae

I n winter, the Orkney islands are battered by strong winds. In 1850, a storm blew the grass from a mound, and uncovered the outline of an ancient stone village! The discovery fascinated landowner William Watt, who started excavating the site.

Watt discovered four of the eight houses at Skara Brae. Further digs in 1928 discovered even more ancient buildings (pictured above). In the 1970s, experts using **radiocarbon dating** found that the settlement was lived in between 3200 BCE and 2200 BCE! Protected by the sand for 4,000 years, the buildings were very well-preserved. Alleyways between the houses still had their original stone slab roofs. Each house has a central fireplace, a bed on either side, and a stone dresser opposite the doorway.

bed

dresser

bed

fireplace

Artifact Facts

A number of carved stone balls were found at the site. Similar balls have been found in Scotland and the Boyne Valley, Ireland. No one knows what the balls were for. They might have been used in a **ritual**.

Skara Brae

Scotland

Ireland

Boyne Valley

Artifacts made from bone, ivory, or teeth were found. These included needles, knives, beads, shovels, bowls, and ivory pins. The pins were similar to ones found in the Boyne Valley. Could these ancient people have traveled all that way?

THE GIANT'S RING

The Giant's Ring is a large circular **enclosure** in Northern Ireland. The enclosure is surrounded by an 11-foot-high (3.5 m) bank. Inside the enclosure is a small tomb. The Giant's Ring was built around 2700 BCE. The site was probably used as a meeting place or as a memorial to the dead. The remains of another nearby circle excavated in the 1700s was said to have contained many bones. Farmers plowing the surrounding fields discovered human bones, also.

Giant's Ring

Artifact Facts

In 1855, a local farmer found another nearby burial chamber while he was digging potatoes. He noticed a broad, flat stone, and when he lifted it he found the entrance to a tomb! Two young farm boys managed to climb inside, where they found an urn full of bones, and three skulls. The bones had been burned before burial, but the skulls had not.

dolmen

First Farmers

In the middle of the Giant's Ring is a tomb known as a **dolmen**. Made up of five upright stones and a large covering stone, it was originally a chambered grave. Dolmens were covered with earth or small stones to form a mound, but these would have been washed away over the years, leaving only the stone "skeleton" of the burial mound.

Archaeologists do not know who built this Giant's Ring dolmen, or why. There are examples of dolmens all over the ancient world. They are believed to be burial chambers, as human remains and **grave goods** are usually found nearby.

The Giant's Ring was not built for protection. Castles were built with the ditch around the outside of their bank walls, rather than having the low area on the inside like the Giant's Ring does. The bank may have originally had a flat top and was a platform for spectators to watch ceremonies.

low ground

bank

AVEBURY CIRCLE

During the time known as the "First Farmers," people began to farm crops and keep animals, and to settle in one place. They made pottery to store food in, and ate more cereals and bread. They also started to build. Enclosures like the Giant's Ring, and **henges** like the one below at Avebury, were built at sites across Britain. A henge is a circle of upright stones or wood. No one really knows what they were for, but they must have taken many people a long time to build, so they must have been very important.

Avebury has three stone circles, one of which is the largest in Europe. It was built around 2600 BCE. Archaeologists believe it was used for some form of ritual or ceremony. In the 1600s, history enthusiasts John Aubrey and William Stukeley recorded the site, which helped modern archaeologists restore it.

Avebury

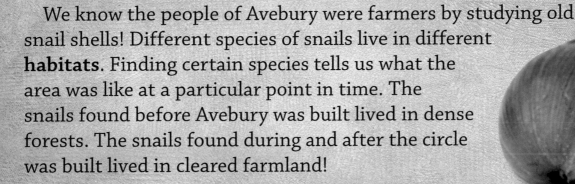

We know the people of Avebury were farmers by studying old snail shells! Different species of snails live in different **habitats**. Finding certain species tells us what the area was like at a particular point in time. The snails found before Avebury was built lived in dense forests. The snails found during and after the circle was built lived in cleared farmland!

In the early 1300s, villagers began to pull down the standing stones and bury them in pits dug next to them. They probably did this because they thought the stones were **pagan** and against their Christian beliefs. One of the stones collapsed on top of one of the men, killing him and trapping his body in the hole dug ready for the falling stone. The villagers stopped the destruction of the circle, perhaps because they feared the death had in some way been a punishment for destroying them.

The Barber Stone

Artifact Facts

In 1938, archaeologists raised the stone and found the body (below). He had a leather pouch holding three silver coins from around 1320, a pair of scissors, and a surgeon's knife. Archaeologists believe he was a traveling barber-surgeon who happened to be there when the stones were toppled.

STONEHENGE

Stonehenge

Stonehenge is an ancient ring of standing stones surrounded by a circular earth bank and ditch. Archaeologists believe it was built sometime between 3000 to 2000 BCE. The earth bank and ditch were made a little earlier. Stonehenge could have been a burial ground from its earliest beginnings, as some **cremated** remains found date from as early as 3000 BCE.

Within the earth banks are 56 pits, known as the Aubrey holes after John Aubrey. They may have held upright timber posts, or they may have held stones.

Some archaeologists believe Stonehenge might have been used as a calendar. The circle is precisely lined up to the direction of the midsummer sunrise, the midwinter sunset, and the movements of the moon!

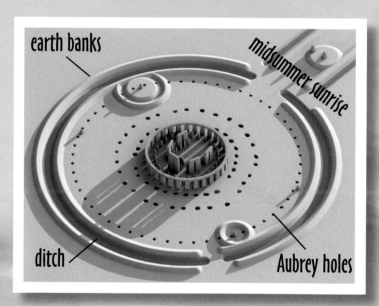

earth banks

midsummer sunrise

ditch

Aubrey holes

A computer image of how Stonehenge might have looked.

Bronze Age

Two different types of stone were used to make the henge. The larger stones are called sarsens. They are up to 30 feet (9 m) tall! They were probably brought from nearby Marlborough Downs. The smaller stones are called bluestones, as they look blue when wet. They may be smaller, but they still weigh up to 4 tons! Bluestones are believed to have come from Wales, 140 miles (225 km) away!

No one knows how the stones got to Stonehenge. They may have been moved along the river on wooden boats, or pulled using sleds made from tree trunks. It is also possible that during the last Ice Age the bluestones were carried by glaciers from Wales, to much closer to Stonehenge.

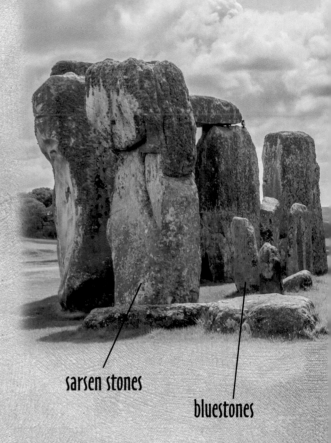

sarsen stones

bluestones

Artifact Facts

This special stone, the Heel Stone, stands away from the main stone circle. If you stood at the center of the circle at sunrise on the summer or winter **solstice**, you would see the Sun rise directly over the Heel Stone. This could be accidental, but it was probably built like that on purpose.

MOUSA BROCH

The Iron Age in Britain was from around 750 BCE to 43 CE. Before this period, tools and weapons had been made from copper and bronze. The Iron Age started when people learned how to get iron from rock using a very hot fire. Iron was harder and stronger than bronze.

Mousa Broch is an Iron Age round tower in the Shetland Isles. It was built around 100 BCE. It stands near the shore. It is a very complex building, with stairs, passages, and even air vents within the walls. The roof was probably built of timber, with a turf, hide, or straw covering.

Could these vents be Iron Age **air conditioning**?

Iron Age brochs look a little like castles. They probably weren't used for defense, though, as there are no wall-top defenses or windows. If an invader lit a fire near the entrance it would easily have smoked out the people inside.

Artifact Facts

A staircase between two stone walls winds around the building to an open walkway at the top. On each floor, between the two outer walls, there are galleries you can walk around. Spaces within the broch's hollow walls were probably used as storage units or guard cells.

Archaeologists think the brochs may have been used as grain stores as well as living spaces. Post-holes in the floor show that posts would once have supported platforms that may have been used for storing grain. Also, they have found evidence the people kept pet cats, which would have helped prevent rats and mice from eating the grain. The hollow walls and air vents may have acted as air conditioning too, making the broch ideal for storage.

On the ground floor there was a central hearth for cooking and a water tank. A low, stone bench ran around the wall.

cell entrance

bench

water tank

THE TOW ROPE

RAF Valley

In 1943, Britain was at war with Germany. William Owen Roberts, head groundsman at RAF Valley, was busy extending the airfield's runway. Fetching peat from a local lake, their truck got stuck in the mud. When the tractor's wire tow rope broke, Roberts remembered he had seen an old chain in the mud. They used the chain over and over that day to pull the lorry out of the mud.

Roberts thought the chain was unusual. It had five very large links. He drew a diagram of it and sent it with a letter to the museum in Cardiff. The museum's curator came immediately by train. He identified it as a 2,000 year-old gang chain, used to connect five slaves or prisoners together by their necks.

The workmen found more treasures. They found iron swords, a trumpet piece, a bronze plaque, a chariot tire, horse bits, and iron tools. Roberts took them all home balanced on the handlebars of his bicycle and posted them to the museum in Cardiff!

the gang chain

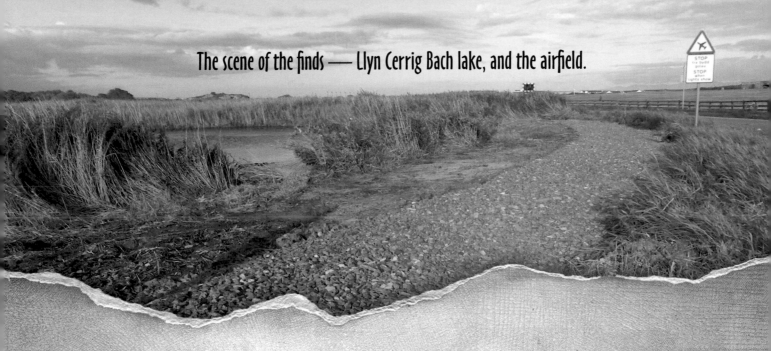

The scene of the finds — Llyn Cerrig Bach lake, and the airfield.

Why were so many priceless things at the bottom of a small lake? Archaeologists believe that the local **Celts** worshiped water gods. They may have thrown precious objects into water to please them. Experts believe they may have offered weapons before or after battle to ask for help, or to thank the gods for victory. Some archaeologists believe that the gifts may have come from one mass offering. Perhaps the Celts saw a Roman army preparing to invade and threw all their precious objects into the lake in the hope of help from their god?

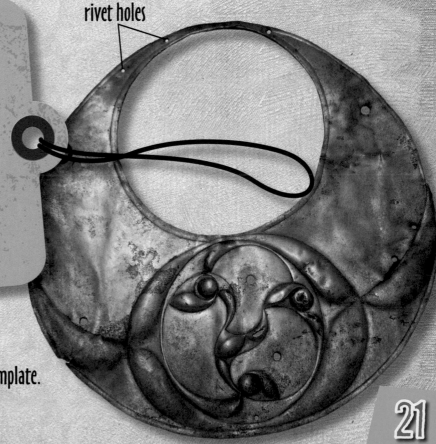

rivet holes

Artifact Facts

This bronze plaque is one of the most important pieces of Iron Age decorated metalwork ever found. The rivet holes mean it was probably attached to something, perhaps the front of a chariot, or a statue.

The plaque's design was made by beating the bronze over a wood template.

OLD SARUM

The abandoned settlement of Old Sarum is on a hill about 2 miles (3 km) north of Salisbury. Archaeologists have found evidence of a settlement there as early as 3,000 BCE. Early hunters and, later, farming communities lived at the site. The Iron Age hillfort was built around 400 BCE, at the crossroads of two well-used trade paths and the River Avon. Enormous banks and ditches were built around the hill. Old Sarum has a double bank with a ditch between the two, and an entrance to the east. It is believed to have been an important city.

Later, in 1003, Old Sarum became home to a mint. A mint is a place where coins are made. The Celts developed the system of standardized coins, naming the king, the mint, and individual maker of each coin. Every few years, new coins would be made to replace the old ones.

A silver coin minted at Old Sarum, bearing the name of King Æthelred, who was King from 978–1013 and 1014–1016.

Old Sarum

Celtic

an Iron Age antler pick

During the Iron Age, hundreds of hillforts were built across Britain. There are two main types of hillforts: a contour fort, where a bank and ditch is dug around an existing hill; and a promontory fort, built on a spur of land surrounded by river or sea.

The Iron Age workers built huge structures using just antler picks and wooden spades! They moved all the rubble and soil using baskets.

A bank and ditch at Old Sarum

A model of how Old Sarum would have looked in the 1300s.

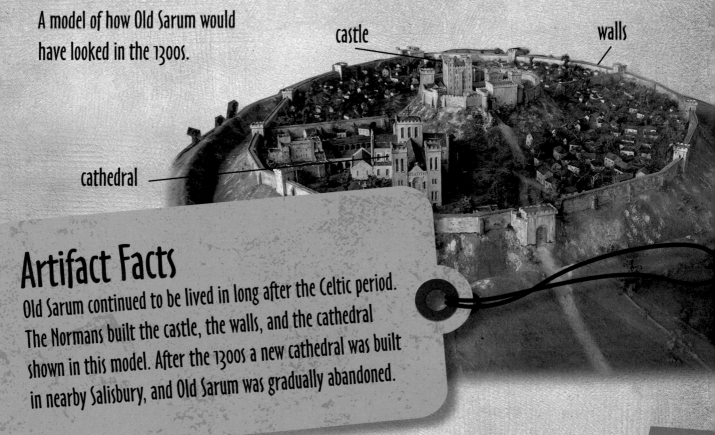

castle

walls

cathedral

Artifact Facts

Old Sarum continued to be lived in long after the Celtic period. The Normans built the castle, the walls, and the cathedral shown in this model. After the 1300s a new cathedral was built in nearby Salisbury, and Old Sarum was gradually abandoned.

CHYSAUSTER

Chysauster

Chysauster is a 2,000-year-old Iron Age settlement. The village is made up of nine stone-walled courtyard houses with their own gardens, and sheds for keeping animals. The houses line a village street. This type of Iron Age settlement is only found in the far south west of Britain. Each house had a central courtyard surrounded by several straw-roofed rooms.

The people were farmers. Archaeologists have found evidence of cereal crops in fields next to the village. The villagers probably kept pigs and goats, too. The houses had hearths for cooking, and stone water channels that acted as guttering to collect rainwater. Archaeologists have also found circular stones known as querns, used for grinding corn.

Rooms off a courtyard at Chysauster

The village street at Chysauster

People lived at Chysauster all during the Roman occupation of Britain, and then abandoned it suddenly. No one is sure why.

At Chysauster there are remains of a fogou. "Fogou" means "cave" in the local language, Cornish. Fogous are found in other places in Britain, too, and known as "souterrains" which means "underground" in French. No one is sure what the underground passages were for. They may have been ritual buildings, hiding places, or places to keep food cold.

The Chysauster fogou was over 52 feet (16 m) long.

Artifact Facts

The main rooms at Chysauster all have a central, flat stone with a hole in the middle, like this one. Archaeologists believe that the hole supported a wooden post that in turn supported a roof made of turf or straw.

HADRIAN'S WALL

Hadrian's Wall

In 43 CE, the Roman Emperor, Claudius, sent an army to invade Britain. He wanted to make Britain part of Rome's empire. You can still see evidence of the Roman invasion in Britain in the ruins of many buildings, forts, roads, and baths.

The Romans never conquered the northern part of Britain. In 122 CE, Emperor Hadrian ordered his soldiers to build a wall to divide the island between Roman and non-Roman areas. The wall ran for 73 miles (117 km) from the west coast to the east coast. It took about 14 years to complete. It was the largest Roman structure ever built!

A milecastle along the wall

A statue of Emperor Hadrian

There were 16 forts built along the wall. Each fort could house 800 soldiers, and had their own prisons, hospitals, bakeries, and stables. Along the wall, a Roman mile (.92 miles, or 1.48 km) apart, were "milecastles." These gateways allowed Roman soldiers to patrol north of Hadrian's Wall. The milecastles were used as customs posts, too, controlling who and what could cross the wall. Between the milecastles, **turrets** allowed soldiers to keep watch over the surrounding countryside.

While a lot of the wall still stands today, some of the stone was taken for road building. A Newcastle town clerk, John Clayton, helped preserve the wall by buying much of the land it stood on, and restoring sections of the wall.

A stretch of Hadrian's Wall crossing the countryside

Artifact Facts

This Roman treasure was found buried near Hadrian's Wall. Experts believe the gold and silver pieces were buried by someone as an offering. Some of the treasure had inscriptions to mother-goddesses. Mother-goddesses represent life, so perhaps they were giving thanks for a good crop. The objects must have belonged to a wealthy person.

ROMAN BATHS

Bath

Bathing was an important part of daily routine for the Romans. They built public bath houses across the Roman Empire. Roman bath houses were a little like a health spa. The people would meet friends, exercise, and bathe there.

The city of Bath was home to a Roman bath house. A natural, hot spring bubbled out of the ground there. The Celts had already built a shrine to the goddess, Sulis, at the spring. When the Romans arrived they named the city "Aquae Sulis" which means "the waters of Sulis." They built their own temple and the luxurious baths. The baths featured a caldarium (hot bath), a tepidarium (warm bath), and a frigidarium (cold bath).

A statue of Sulis found at the temple at Bath.

All that remains of the original Roman baths are the lowest levels of stonework near the water's edge. The newer abbey towers stand behind the baths.

When the Romans left Britain, in the 400s, the temples and baths were abandoned. Only the fallen temple to Sulis marked the ancient site. The town continued to grow, though. Christian buildings were built on the ruins of the Roman temple. In the early 1600s Bath became very fashionable. Wealthy families began to visit the natural springs, which were believed to cure illnesses. While building new baths for the visitors, the ancient Roman baths were rediscovered.

Thousands of Roman coins were found in the baths, presumably offerings to the goddess, Sulis. In 2007, more than 30,000 Roman coins were found by archaeologists working in Bath, but these were probably a hidden hoard due to local unrest.

Artifact Facts

Around 130 curse tablets like this one were found at the Roman baths. Curse tablets are metal sheets with inscribed messages asking the gods to help get revenge. Many of the curse tablets ask for revenge on people who have stolen their clothes while they were bathing!

This tablet asks "May he who has stolen Vilbia from me become as liquid as water!" Perhaps Vilbia was a wife, or servant?

GLOSSARY

air conditioning A mechanism to cool air inside a building.

archaeologists Scientists that study past human life, fossils, monuments and tools left by ancient peoples.

Celts Early European people who lived in the British Isles, France, Spain, and parts of Asia.

cremated Burned a dead body to ashes.

dolmen A megalithic tomb with a large flat stone laid on upright ones, found in Britain and France.

enclosure An area that is surrounded by a barrier.

excavated Uncovered an area by digging away the earth.

extinct No longer existing.

flint A hard gray rock, flaked or ground in ancient times to form a tool or weapon.

grave goods Useful and valuable objects left in prehistoric and ancient graves, probably intended for use in the afterlife.

habitats The kind of land where an animal or a plant naturally lives.

henges Prehistoric monuments made of a circular ditch inside a circular bank.

Homo antecessor An extinct human species (or subspecies) dating from 800,000 to 1.2 million years ago.

long barrow A prehistoric earth mound, usually rectangular in shape, and believed to have been used as a tomb.

mudflats A stretch of muddy land left uncovered at low tide.

pagan A person holding religious beliefs other than those of the main world religions.

radiocarbon dating A technique for working out the age of organic materials, such as wood.

ritual A special series of actions done for reasons of faith.

solstice The times in the year when the sun reaches its highest or lowest point in the sky at noon, marked by the longest and shortest days.

turrets Little towers.

FURTHER INFORMATION

Books

Frith, Alex and McNee, Ian. *Prehistoric Britain*. London, UK: Usborne Publishing Ltd, 2014.

Hebditch, Felicity. *Roman Britain* (Britain Through the Ages). London, UK: Cherrytree Books, 2015.

Manning, Mick. *Secrets of Stonehenge*. London, UK: Frances Lincoln Children's Books, 2013.

Martell, Hazel Mary. *Celts* (Britain Through the Ages). London, UK: Cherrytree Books, 2015.

Due to the changing nature of Internet links, PowerKids Press has developed an online list of websites related to the subject of this book. This site is updated regularly. Please use this link to access the list:

www.powerkidslinks.com/ACC/Britain

INDEX